Ben Wicks

AND COMPANY

AND COMPANY

The Third Cartoon Treasury

BY BEN AND VINCENT WICKS

The cartoons reproduced in this Treasury include material from the collections of York University and The National Archives of Canada.

Canadian Cataloguing in Publication Data

Wicks, Ben
Wicks & Company

ISBN 0-7710-8838-8

1. Canadian wit and humor, Pictorial. I. Wicks, Vincent. II. Title.

NC1449.W5A4 1990 741.5'971 C90-095273-3

Printed and bound in Canada

McClelland & Stewart, Inc.
The Canadian Publishers
481 University Avenue
Toronto, Ontario
M5G 2E9

WIFE
SON
© 1989 Southam Syndicate
WICKS

"No thanks, I'm trying to quit."

"A man with a beard and a lady with a baby? They checked out yesterday."

"You've forgotten to put the computer out."

QUICK BILL, OLLIE NORTH'S ON T.V.
© SOUTHAM SYN.

BOY, HE CAN REALLY TALK UP A STORM, CAN'T HE?
4/7/88

IT'S A LOT OF PATRIOTIC DRIVEL IF YOU ASK ME
HEY— HE'S NOT ASKING YOU TO SING 'STARS AND STRIPES, FOREVER'

AND NOW I'D LIKE YOU ALL TO JOIN ME IN SINGING 'STARS AND STRIPES FOREVER'
WICKS

WHAT ARE YOU WATCHING, BILL?

THE STUDENT MARCHES IN BEIJING
6/20/89

© 1989 Southam Syndicate

WARN ME BEFORE YOU SWITCH TO THE REPORT FROM LEBANON
WICKS

WELL DAN, I'M GOING TO LET YOU MAKE THIS DECISION
© 1989 Southam Syndicate

WELL, LET'S SEE . . .

. . . LET'S START WITH A BOWL OF CHEERIOS EACH
6/15/89

NO DAN, THIS IS LUNCH — TURN THE PAGE
WICKS

"Here's how it goes. I start singing, 'Row, row, row your boat,' and as soon as I say 'boat', you start . . ."

"Section 84 wants air conditioning."

"Are you telling me you think the shape of something God made is all wrong?"

LISTEN BILL, WE'VE GOT TO TAKE A STAND
© 1989 Southam Syndicate
THESE KID GANGS ARE OUT OF CONTROL – WE'VE DECIDED TO BAND TOGETHER
WELL, IF THE WORLD EVER NEEDED THE MICKEY MOUSE CLUB IT'S NOW
4/29/89
THE RAT PATROL, BILL!
SORRY

JUST HOW MUCH OF A DISTURBANCE ARE LOW LEVEL FLIGHTS FOR THE INNU... FOR A REPORT WE GO TO LABRADOR...

WELL PETER...
'BROOM, BOOM'

'BOOM BROOM, BOOM'
5/19/89

THANKS A LOT...
'BROOM, BOOM'
© 1989 Southam Syndicate

I MUST SAY HE'S REALLY SETTLED DOWN SINCE THE OLYMPICS ENDED

IT WAS ALL HE TALKED ABOUT DAY IN AND DAY OUT
© 1988 Southam Syndicate

IT REALLY IS NICE TO HAVE A BREAK FROM ALL THAT SPORTS
10/11/88

'AND GRETZKY STEPS OUT ON TO THE ICE!'

"He can't come to the phone now. He's trying to quit smoking."

"186532 got into the fax room and is somewhere in South America."

"He claims he can taste PCBs."

"It's no good, Mona. We're going to have to try something else."

"Here's one. Complete with turrets, a moat, and drawbridge. No reasonable offer refused."

"And over here we have the oldest building, dating from March 1989."

"Perestroika or no perestroika, I still say this is demeaning for the KGB."

"All ashore that's going ashore!"

"Are you or have you ever been a concerned citizen?"

I'M FED UP WITH THIS RIGHT WING TREND IN WESTERN POLITICS-

-THATCHER, MULRONEY, BUSH - THEY DON'T GIVE A HOOT ABOUT THE WORKING POOR-
© 1989 Southam Syndicate

- THE HOMELESS, SINGLE MOTHERS TRYING TO FIND DAY CARE
5/24/89

BUT DO THEY MAKE THE TRAINS RUN ON TIME?
WHY DON'T YOU TAKE A LONG GOOSE STEP OFF A SHORT PLATFORM!
WICKS

THE HONEYMOON IS OVER GEORGE- WE'VE GOT TO PROVE TO AMERICA THAT YOU CAN HANDLE THE JOB-

- THAT YOU'VE GOT THE RIGHT STUFF

YOU'RE ABSOLUTELY RIGHT — I'M GOING TO FLY THAT MISSION TO MARS MYSELF!

LET ME START AGAIN GEORGE
© 1989 Southam Syndicate
WICKS

IS RON IN THE OFFICE?
YES, MR. BUSH

GREAT, I WANT TO GET TOGETHER FOR ONE LAST CHAT

WELL, HE'S SLEEPING AT THE MOMENT, MR. BUSH

WONDERFUL- THAT'S JUST HOW I'D WANT TO REMEMBER HIM
WICKS

"Nothing for my friend. He's driving."

© 1989 Southam Syndicate

"You wanted a second opinion?"

"Tell you what – you go back to your chair and I promise I'll discuss your raise on December 26th."

I CAN'T GET OVER THE POLLUTION THIS SUMMER—

—THE SMOG IS SO THICK YOU CAN'T SEE THREE FEET IN FRONT OF YOUR FACE

HERE, TAKE MY HAND, MAVIS
IT'S YOUR EYES NOT THE AIR THAT'S THE PROBLEM

© 1989 Southam Syndicate

ISN'T IT NICE THAT GAY PEOPLE NOW HAVE THE RIGHT TO BE TREATED AS A FAMILY UNIT

IT WILL BE SUCH A RELIEF TO YOUR SISTER'S SON OLIVER
© 1989 Southam Syndicate
5/12/89

WHY WILL IT BE SUCH A RELIEF, TO MY SISTER'S SON OLIVER?
WICKS

WHERE'S MY FALSE BEARD, MILA?
IT'S IN THE BEDROOM
SUSSEX DRIVE
AND MY DARK GLASSES AND RUBBER NOSE?
ON THE HALL TABLE
SUSSEX DRIVE

THE NEXT TIME YOU RELEASE A BUDGET THE KIDS AND I ARE LEAVING TOWN FOR A MONTH
SUSSEX DRIVE
© 1989 Southam Syndicate
5/17/89

FINE—NOW WHAT DID YOU NEED FROM THE STORE?
SUSSEX DRIVE
WICKS

"Well, I must say I never expected to see *you* up here!"

"I'm afraid it's phaechromocytoma. Or, to put it in layman's terms, about $175 a letter."

"Whoopee, it's land – we're saved!"

"He won't let me watch the baseball game."

"Then Snow White caught the prince playing around, so she dumped him for a commoner and lived happily ever after."

"And now to the bulk of my estate..."

"Every time I see a mailman, I go crazy."

YOU KNOW THAT 'SAVE THE GREY SEAL' CAMPAIGN IS PARTLY RESPONSIBLE FOR OUR DEPLETED COD STOCKS

THE SEAL POPULATION HAS EXPLODED AND THEY ARE EATING UP STOCKS BY THE BOAT LOAD
© 1989 Southam Syndicate

BUT WHAT CAN YOU DO ABOUT IT?
A NEW CAMPAIGN THAT'S WHAT

SAVE THE COD

WHAT'S UP GEORGE?
I THINK MAYBE IT'S TIME I DISTANCED MYSELF FROM YOU MR. PRESIDENT

WHAT DO YOU MEAN?
YOU KNOW- APPEAR MORE INDEPENDENT- GET OUT FROM UNDER YOUR SHADOW
6/25/88

YOU'RE STANDING IN MY SHADOW?
© 1988 Southam Syndicate

I AM- SORRY ABOUT THAT- MAYBE IF I STAND HERE- OR MAYBE HERE- OR HOW ABOUT...
WICKS

I DON'T KNOW ABOUT GEORGE BUSH
© 1988 Southam Syndicate

I GET THE FEELING HE'S HIDING SOMETHING
8/12/88

LIKE WHAT?
CHARISMA- PERSONALITY- INTELLECT- A SENSE OF HUMOR

THAT'S HIS C.I.A. TRAINING
WICKS

"God will get you for this, Noah!"

"Okay. Now let's try that again . . . say ahhhh!"

"You promised me sharks. No one said anything about the Niagara River."

© 1989 Southam Syndicate
WICKS
"Run for your lives – it's a takeover!"

MR. JOHNSON, WOULD YOU SAY STEROIDS HELPED INCREASE YOUR SPEED?

BEFORE I ANSWER THAT COULD I GET A DRINK
THERE'S A WATER FOUNTAIN JUST OUTSIDE THIS ROOM

GO AHEAD MR. JOHNSON GET YOUR DRINK?
5/5/89
© 1989 Southam Syndicate

I JUST DID!
WICKS

WHAT'S ALL THIS MONEY DOING IN YOUR SOCK, BILL?

I MADE SURE I WAS PREPARED FOR THE WILSON BUDGET
© 1989 Southam Syndicate

LET THIS BE A LESSON IN THE IMPORTANCE OF PLANNING AHEAD, MAVIS
5/15/89

CHECK MY PANTYHOSE— TOP LEFT DRAWER!

"Hey! Is anybody here?"

"Listen, I'd better go. I think there's someone waiting to use the phone."

"I can forgive you losing the race, but the horse?"

© 1990 Southam Syndicate
Wicks

"To which you replied, 'Oh yeah, well how would you like to step outside?' Mr. Evans seconded the proposal."

ARE YOU COMING IN SWIMMING GRANDPA?

ACTUALLY I FORGOT MY SWIM TRUNKS
© 1989 Southam Syndicate

I THOUGHT YOU MIGHT HAVE SO I BROUGHT AN EXTRA PAIR
7/3/89

MY HERO
Wicks

WHEN ARE WE GOING TO GET SOME ACTION ON ACID RAIN?

BRIAN'S DOING EVERYTHING HE CAN TO GET GEORGE BUSH TO... TRY... AND....
© 1989 Southam Syndicate

Z
Z
Z
6/1/89

THAT'S JUST GREAT — HIS OWN RHETORIC PUTS HIM TO SLEEP
Wicks

"You never take me anywhere."

QUICK-
EVERYBODY
OUTSIDE

RUDOLPH'S NOSE
MUST HAVE
BLOWN A FUSE
OR SANTA'S SLEIGH
OVERTURNED
OR SOMETHING
© 1988 Southam Syndicate

THERE ARE
CHRISTMAS
PRESENTS
ALL OVER
THE LAWN
12/24/88

COULDN'T YOU
JUST PUT THEM
UNDER THE TREE
LIKE EVERYBODY
ELSE?

AUDREY McLAUGHLIN'S
GETTING A LOT OF
SUPPORT IN HER
RACE FOR THE
N.D.P. LEADERSHIP-

-I THINK
SHE WOULD
BE
EXCELLENT-
HA
© 1989 Southam Syndicate

-IT'S ABOUT TIME
THIS COUNTRY HAD
A PARTY LEADER
WITH A WOMAN'S
PERSPECTIVE-
HA HA
9/6/89

-SOMEONE
LIKE MAGGIE
THATCHER
WICKS

LOOK MAVIS,
IT'S MICHAEL
WILSON
6/7/89

WHERE ARE
YOU GOING?
© 1989 Southam Syndicate

I'VE GOT A
BASKET OF
TOMATOES
I WAS SAVING
FOR THIS
MOMENT
WICKS

"Endangered species first!"

I CAN'T GET OVER BREZHNEV'S SON-IN-LAW ACCEPTING ALL THOSE BRIBES-
10/3/88

-THE MAN ACCUMULATED A SMALL FORTUNE

© 1988 Southam Syndicate
I'LL TELL YA, MAVIS- THERE'S STILL HOPE FOR THOSE RUSSIANS!
WICKS
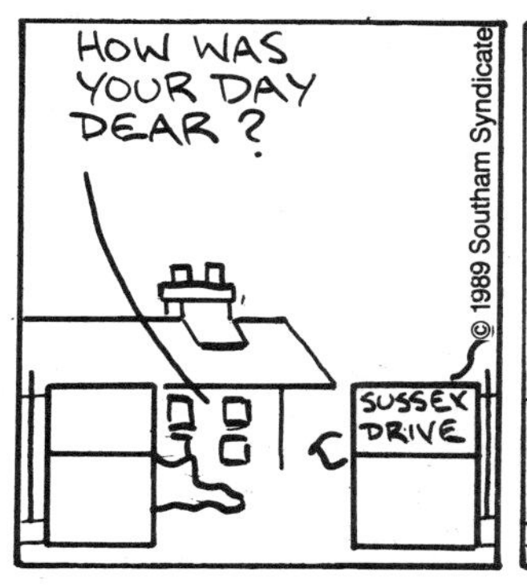
HOW WAS YOUR DAY DEAR?
© 1989 Southam Syndicate
SUSSEX DRIVE

LOUSY!
SUSSEX DRIVE

COME INTO THE DEN- I'VE GOT A LITTLE SURPRISE FOR YOU
SUSSEX DRIVE
9/11/89

A FRESH 8X10 OF ERIC NIELSEN FOR MY DART BOARD- MILA YOU THINK OF EVERYTHING
SUSSEX DRIVE
WICKS

I SURE HOPE ALL THESE ENVIRONMENTAL CLEAN UPS WORK

IT WOULD BE SO NICE TO PASS ON A CLEAN PLANET TO OUR CHILDREN
© 1989 Southam Syndicate
7/11/89

HI GRANDMA
HI GRANDPA

AND TEACH THEM HOW TO KEEP IT THAT WAY
WICKS

THINGS SURE ARE QUIET-

-NOTHING HAPPENING- NO DECISIONS BEING MADE-
© 1989 Southam Syndicate

-NONE OF THE BIG PROBLEMS THAT FACE THIS COUNTRY BEING SOLVED
3/2/89

JUST BUSINESS AS USUAL I GUESS?
WICKS

YOU LOOK A LITTLE CONFUSED TODAY, ED
I'M THINKING ABOUT THE N.D.P POSITION ON N.A.T.O-
ED BROAD-BENT

-SHOULD WE STAY 'IN' BECAUSE IT'S 'IN TO BE IN'- OR SHOULD WE GET OUT EVEN THOUGH IT'S 'IN TO BE IN'-
ED BROAD-BENT
©T.SS

-AND IF WE WERE OUT COULD WE GET 'IN'- OR EVEN IF WE WERE 'IN' WOULD WE BE OUT
ED BROAD-BENT

SHOULD WE STAY IN OR GO OUT FOR DINNER?
ED BROAD-BENT
WICKS

BOY, ANOTHER REALLY COLD MORNING- I'M FREEZING

WHAT HAPPENED TO THE GREEN-HOUSE EFFECT THIS FEELS LIKE AN ICE AGE

CAN YOU PASS ME MY TEETH
© 1988 Southam Syndicate

HAVE YOU GOT AN ICE PICK?
1/7/89
WICKS

LISTEN GEORGE I WANT YOU TO KNOW I'M HOPPING MAD ABOUT THIS CLEAN AIR BILL —
— NOW YOU MADE SOME PROMISES AND I EXPECT YOU TO KEEP THEM
WHAT DO YOU THINK MILA?
I LOVE IT — IT'S TOUGH
REALLY — SO WHERE SHOULD I WATER IT DOWN?
SUSSEX DRIVE
© 1989 Southam Syndicate
8/25/89
Wicks

HEY, MAVIS, YOU'RE NOT GOING TO BELIEVE THIS —
© 1989 Southam Syndicate

— OUR NEPHEW AND A LOAD OF HIS LITTLE FRIENDS ARE BLOCKING THE DRIVEWAY — I CAN'T PARK

THEY'RE PLAYING GOVERNMENT AND INDIANS
9/4/89

NOW TAKE YOUR BRIEFCASE OUT — TELL THEM THEY CAN'T HAVE THEIR LAND AND LET'S SEE WHAT HAPPENS

HASN'T IT BEEN A WONDERFUL SUMMER, BRIAN
SUSSEX DRIVE
© 1989 Southam Syndicate

WHAT PLANET HAVE YOU BEEN LIVING ON —

— THE PRESS HAVE RUINED ME — THEY MADE ME LOOK LIKE AN IDIOT ALL SUMMER
9/5/89

AND WE WERE SO CAREFUL NOT TO LET THAT GET OUT
WELL SOMEBODY LEAKED IT!
Wicks

"I'm afraid it's the result of the greenhouse effect."

"He's with someone important. Would you mind waiting?"

"There, there, dear, his time had come."

CAN YOU SHOW ME HOW TO THROW A JAVELIN, GRANDPA

A LITTLE INSPIRATION FROM THE OLYMPICS, EH?
© 1988 Southam Syndicate

WELL YOU JUST HOLD IT LIKE THIS- TAKE A RUN- AND...
9/20/88

YOU KNOW- I WAS THINKING- WHEN WAS THE LAST TIME YOU AND I WENT OUT FOR DINNER?
WICKS

HAVE YOU SEEN MY FISHING ROD, MAVIS? -
© 1988 Southam Syndicate

- FRED HIGGINS WANTS TO TAKE ME DOWN TO THE LAKE TO DO SOME FISHING -
8/9/88

- WHO KNOWS MAYBE I'LL CATCH A BIG MOUTH BASS
WICKS

THAT WOULD BE NICE- EVERY MAN NEEDS A PET

WHERE DID THESE APPLES COME FROM?
I'M NOT SURE

© 1989 Southam Syndicate
HERE HAVE SOME GRAPES
4/5/89

YEAH RIGHT!
WHAT ABOUT A NICE PIECE OF CHICKEN?

HOW LONG DID YOU COOK IT?
I GIVE UP!
WICKS

"There's a threatened takeover bid."

"Evans, the trouble with you is you're getting too big for your britches."

"Your husband's right. It really is late and we should be going."

"Cough, cough, cough!"

© 1989 Southam Syndicate
Wicks

"Ring-g-g-g..."

IT SURE IS GETTING TOUGH TO MAKE ENDS MEET
© 1989 Southam Syndicate

WHAT'S THAT MAVIS ?
6/14/89

IT'S OUR GRANDSON'S COLLEGE FUND

I'M SURE I HEARD THE BOY SAY HE WANTED TO BE A HOCKEY PLAYER
WICKS

THIS IS IT, MAVIS – THE START OF A NEW YEAR

TIME TO PUT THE PAST BEHIND US – TIME TO LOOK TO THE FUTURE
1/2/89

OUT WITH THE OLD AND IN WITH THE NEW
© 1988 Southam Syndicate

VERY FUNNY, MAVIS
WICKS

WICKS
"It's 10 p.m. Do you know where your husband is?"

NOW THIS IS EXCITING –

– THE U.S. WANTS TO PUT A MAN ON MARS

AND I'VE GOT JUST THE MAN FOR THE JOB
8/8/89

YOU CRACK ME UP, MAVIS
© 1989 Southam Syndicate
WICKS

I WONDER WHO THIS LETTER IS FROM

I WON THE TRAVEL CONTEST –
I WON
I WON!
7/12/89

I'VE NEVER WON A CONTEST IN MY LIFE – THIS IS UNBELIEVABLE!
© 1989 Southam Syndicate

TWO ECONOMY CLASS TICKETS TO BEIJING
WICKS

"My fellow East Germans . . ."

"I'm afraid Mr. Evans is in a meeting."

"It's your mother."

WHEN IS THE GOVERNMENT GOING TO RESOLVE THIS ABORTION ISSUE?

WHEN THEY COME TO THE CONCLUSION THAT A WOMANS BODY IS HER OWN
8/1/89

AND WHOSE BODY DOES THE FETUS BELONG TO?

IF YOU WANT TO GET INTO THIS, I'M PRIMED!
WICKS
© 1989 Southam Syndicate

WE'VE GOT TO START TIGHTENING OUR BELTS–
© 1989 Southam Syndicate

THERE'S TALK OF A RECESSION AGAIN, BILL
8/24/89

TALK'S CHEAP!

WELL THEN– YOU'LL BE ABLE TO AFFORD TO EAT THOSE WORDS
WICKS

THE PRICE OF HOMES IS JUST GETTING RIDICULOUS

WHERE ARE YOUNG PEOPLE SUPPOSED TO FIND A DOWN PAYMENT

I'M GLAD YOU BROUGHT THAT UP, DAD
© 1988 Southam Syndicate
1/4/89

ME AND MY BIG MOUTH
WICKS

"Did he say anything about polluting the atmosphere?"

BILL, THERE'S A BIG FAT 'VOTE P.C.' SIGN ON OUR LAWN

WHAT- HOW DID THAT GET THERE?
VOTE P.C
11/18/88

I DON'T KNOW- YOU TELL ME
DIVINE INTERVENTION?

NO- I'D CALL IT A NATURAL DISASTER!
WICKS

I'M GLAD YOU COULD ALL MAKE IT

WE HAVE TO DECIDE WHAT TO GET JOHN TURNER FOR CHRISTMAS
12/12/88

HOW ABOUT A JOB?

HOW DID YOU GET IN HERE, CRETIEN?
WICKS

BRIAN WOULDN'T SELL THIS COUNTRY SHORT, MAVIS - HE'S NOT AS CLOSE TO RON AS THE MEDIA MAKES OUT

BRIAN KEEPS AN INTELLIGENT DISTANCE SO HE'S ABLE TO MAKE UNBIASED DECISIONS ON FREE TRADE
11/19/88

WE'RE GETTING OFF NEAR THE PARLIAMENT BUILDINGS DRIVER

NO PROBLEM- WE JUST PASSED RONALD REAGAN'S BEST FRIEND'S HOUSE
WICKS

"If the Rolling Stones can tour at their age, why can't we?"

"Where do you think I get the money to fight crime?"

"I'm just doing China now, so I'll be home in an hour."

"Then the wicked witch gave Snow White an apple covered with Alar."

"I don't care how old he is in human years, he's still under age."

"Your brother up the street says you're a phoney."

"Sure you can go out on the tiles tonight. We've only got nine lives to live."

"Slow down . . . You're swerving all over the street . . . watch out for that curb . . . You're walking too fast . . ."

IT SURE IS STRANGE
WHAT IS?
© 1989 Southam Syndicate

ED AND JOHN BOTH RETIRING AT ABOUT THE SAME TIME

I GUESS THEY JUST DIDN'T WANT TO LIVE IN THE SHADOW OF THE GREAT ONE ANYMORE
6/2/89

GRETZKY?
LOOK AT MY FACE, MAVIS— I'M NOT LAUGHING
WICKS

HOW LONG ARE YOU GOING TO KEEP THIS UP, MAVIS?

YOU'VE GOT TO TALK TO ME SOMETIME
© 1989 Southam Syndicate
5/23/89

I WASN'T THE ONLY PERSON WHO VOTED FOR THEM

AND HOW COULD I HAVE KNOWN THEY'D BRING IN A BUDGET LIKE THIS!
WICKS

I KNOW YOU FEEL BAD ABOUT JOHN LEAVING, MAVIS-
© 1989 Southam Syndicate

- BUT DON'T YOU THINK YOU'VE SHED ENOUGH TEARS...

... FOR THAT BIG LOSER...
5/26/89

WHAT DID YOU SAY?
YOU SHOULD BLOW YOUR HOOTER
WICKS

THIS COUNTRY WAS JOINED COAST TO COAST BY RAIL
ARE WE GOING TO SIT HERE AND LET MR. MULRONEY DRIVE THE LAST SPIKE IN VIA'S COFFIN—
—ARE YOU GOING TO LET THAT CHATTANOOGA CHUMP RAILROAD YOU AGAIN?
JOHN, WAKE UP— YOU'RE SPEECH WALKING AGAIN!
J.T.
© 1989 Southam Syndicate
22/4/89
WICKS

THERE'S A REPRESENTATIVE FOR THE EAST COAST FISHERMEN HERE, MR. PRIME MINISTER

TA DA' I'M SUPER LOBSTER— LET'S TALK COD QUOTAS!
© 1989 Southam Syndicate

IT'S A GUY IN A LOBSTER SUIT, SIR!
6/8/89

I CAN SEE THAT— RUN AND FIND ME A BIG POT AND A BIB
WICKS

SO YOU QUIT SMOKING EH, EARL?
AT THOSE PRICES IT COULD PUT A GUY ON WELFARE—

—AND WITH ALL THE CUTS TO SOCIAL ASSISTANCE WHO KNOWS WHAT COULD HAPPEN
© 1989 Southam Syndicate

ANOTHER MAN SAVED BY THE GOVERNMENT—
5/22/89

—MULRONEY CERTAINLY MOVES IN STRANGE WAYS, EH, EARL?
WICKS

BEAUTY PARLOR
©1990 Southam Syndicate
WICKS
"Nice try!"

MY GOD!
WHAT'S THE MATTER?
IT SAYS HERE THE GREENHOUSE EFFECT COULD DESTROY LIFE AS WE KNOW IT
© 1988 Southam Syndicate
HOW LONG WILL IT TAKE?
70 YEARS
PUT THE KETTLE ON, MAVIS
7/28/88
WICKS

SO WHO'S GOING TO SUCCEED JOHN TURNER, MAVIS?

I'LL GIVE YOU A HINT – STRONG AND OUTSPOKEN –
6/3/89

– AGGRESSIVE, STUBBORN AND DOWNRIGHT TOUGH
© 1989 Southam Syndicate

YOU REALLY THINK SHEILA COPPS' CHANCES ARE THAT GOOD?
WICKS

I'M PROBABLY A LITTLE BIT RUSTY
© 1989 Southam Syndicate

HERE COMES THE PITCH
6/6/89

WHERE DID YOU COME FROM MR. WILSON?– BOBBY TAKE THE BALL OUT OF MR. WILSON'S MOUTH!
WICKS

IT CERTAINLY WOULD BE NICE IF THE GOVERNMENT TOOK MORE INTEREST IN ORGANIC FARMING–

–I'M SURE THERE ARE MANY PEOPLE WHO WOULD LOVE TO EAT FOOD NOT CONTAMINATED BY PESTICIDES
© 1988 Southam Syndicate
6/15/88

YEAH RIGHT– I'M GOING TO GET RID OF THOSE ANTS IN THE KITCHEN, MAVIS
THANKS BILL

STOMP
STOMP
STOMP
WE CAN DO WITHOUT YOUR SARCASM BILL!
WICKS

SCIENTISTS SAY THE GREENHOUSE EFFECT HAS STARTED
© 1988 Southam Syndicate

IT'S GOING TO KEEP GETTING HOTTER AND HOTTER,
WHAT'S GOING TO HAPPEN TO MY GARDEN?
7/16/88

IT'LL BE BAKED TO A SCORCHED, DRY, ARID WASTELAND –

–THAT NEVER NEEDS WEEDING
WICKS

"Did you tell them we're willing to replace every tree we destroy with a plastic tree?"

IT'S NOT WORTH LIVING ANY MORE

DO ME A FAVOR- BUY A GUN AND SHOOT ME

PUT ME OUT OF MY MISERY
11/4/88

FOR CRYING OUT LOUD BILL, IT'S ONLY A POLL
WICKS

BRIAN, GEORGE HERE
HOW ARE YOU GEORGE?

I WAS WONDERING IF I COULD INTEREST YOU IN A PUPPY OR TWO
© 1989 Southam Syndicate

WHAT'S THE MATTER GEORGE, HAVING A LITTLE TROUBLE WITH THE OLD PAPER TRAINING
6/9/89

I DIDN'T PHONE YOU TO TALK ABOUT DAN QUAYLE, BRIAN!
WICKS

WE'VE GOT TO IMPROVE OUR IMAGE-

-PEOPLE ARE STARTING TO QUESTION THE INTEGRITY OF THIS GOVERNMENT
© 1989 Southam Syndicate

MAYBE WE SHOULD JUST START TELLING THEM THE TRUTH
6/10/89

I CERTAINLY HOPE WE HAVEN'T COME TO THAT
WICKS

"He sent me a valentine, knowing I hadn't sent him one. Isn't that mental cruelty?"

"The Big Cheese is no longer with us."

"I'm sorry, no children allowed."

HA HA HA
YOU'RE NOT GOING TO BELIEVE THIS MR. TRAVERS -

- WE MIXED UP YOUR X-RAYS WITH YOUR GRANDSON'S -
© 1989 Southam Syndicate
9/15/89

- I WAS JUST ABOUT TO COME IN HERE AND TELL YOU TO RUN 10 MILES A DAY -

- I MEAN YOU'RE PROBABLY HAVING TROUBLE GETTING TO THE MAIL BOX AND BACK
WICKS

HEY DAD, BILLY AND HIS PARENTS ARE GOING CAMPING IN P.E.I. -
SUSSEX DRIVE

- BILLY'S DAD WANTS TO KNOW IF WE'D CARE TO JOIN THEM
SUSSEX DRIVE
© 1989 Southam Syndicate

THAT BILLY'S DAD HAS QUITE A SENSE OF HUMOR
SUSSEX DRIVE
8/22/89

- I DON'T THINK I'LL BE SETTING FOOT IN P.E.I AGAIN IN THIS LIFETIME
SUSSEX DRIVE
WICKS

GEORGE, IT'S YOUR FREE TRADE BUDDY BRIAN
WHAT'S UP GOVERNOR?

GOVERNOR?
WHAT?
© 1989 Southam Syndicate

YOU CALLED ME GOVERNOR
I DID?
2/14/89

YES YOU DID
HA HA, JUST A FIGURE OF SPEECH, BRIAN
WICKS

"Come on in, the water's fine."

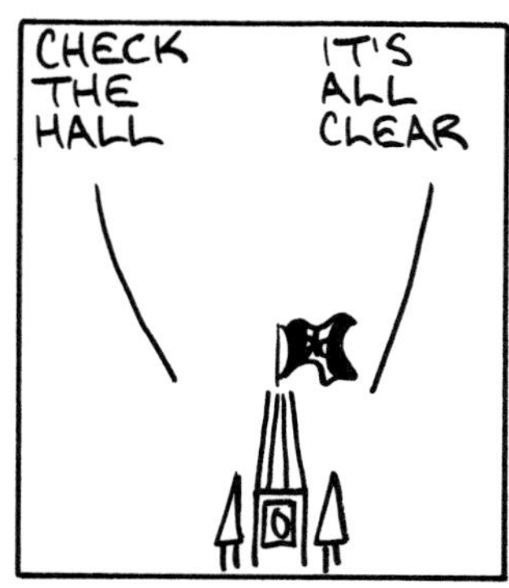
CHECK THE HALL
IT'S ALL CLEAR

PUT ON THE BEARD
BUT IT ITCHES

DON'T GIVE ME A HARD TIME
I'M NOT SITTING IN THAT WHEEL CHAIR
6/22/89
© 1989 Southam Syndicate

LOOK MICHAEL DO YOU WANT TO GO OUT FOR LUNCH OR NOT?
ALL RIGHT, BRIAN
WICKS

I DON'T THINK I CAN TAKE IT, MILA
SUSSEX DRIVE

BEING POPULAR ISN'T EVERYTHING, BRIAN
SUSSEX DRIVE
© 1989 Southam Syndicate

EVEN THE DOG IGNORES ME
SUSSEX DRIVE
7/1/89

DON'T BE SILLY — HE NEVER LIKED YOU
SUSSEX DRIVE

HAS ANYBODY SEEN OUR SECRET SPENDING REPORT?—

— I LEFT IT HERE ON MY DESK BUT IT SEEMS TO HAVE DISAPPEARED
© 1989 Southam Syndicate

I TOOK IT HOME WITH ME LAST NIGHT, BRIAN, SO I COULD READ IT COMING IN ON THE BUS AND I...
6/23/89

...MUST HAVE LEFT IT ON THE BUS
GRAB HIM BY THE LEGS AND OPEN THAT WINDOW!
WICKS

"Wait! It might be on the endangered species list."

SO, MAGGIE THATCHER ARRIVES TOMORROW EH, BILL?
6/21/88

I KNOW— I DREAMT SHE AND I WERE MAROONED ON A DESERT ISLAND

HERE— YOU CAN DO THE DISHES!
© 1988 Southam Syndicate

MAVIS— THAT'S EXACTLY WHAT SHE SAID!
I HAVEN'T SEEN THAT LOOK IN HIS EYES FOR YEARS
WICKS

WHAT'S C.S.I.S DOING SPYING ON THE INUIT AND OTHER NATIVE GROUPS—

IT WOULD BE NICE IF THE GOVERNMENT PUT THAT KIND OF TIME AND ENERGY INTO SOLVING INDIAN PROBLEMS
7/8/89

MAYBE I'LL START A LITTLE COVERT OPERATION AND FIND OUT EXACTLY WHAT C.S.I.S IS UP TO

DID YOU HEAR THAT GUYS?
© 1989 Southam Syndicate
WICKS

POOR OLD VANDER ZALM MUST BE THE MOST UNPOPULAR POLITICIAN IN THE COUNTRY

HA HA
HA HA

BESIDES MULRONEY THAT IS
YEAH, BESIDES MULRONEY THAT...
7/14/89

...VERY FUNNY MAVIS!
© 1989 Southam Syndicate
WICKS

"Those bloody agnostics with their spray cans again."

"Want to neck?"

"I thought they'd never leave."

"I think it's a crank call. Some woman says she can't live without you."

"Beats me what he sees in her."

SPOT THE POPE CONTEST
P
P
P
P
P
© 1989 Southam Syndicate
"And the winner is Gabriel, with his answer, 'The Pope is in Finland'."

THERE'S A PICTURE OF PATRICIA STARR ON PAGE 3
© 1989 Southam Syndicate

BOY, THIS INVESTIGATION HAS REALLY TAKEN ITS TOLL -

- SHE'S GROWN A BEARD - SHE'S WEARING WEIRD CLOTHES AND SHE'S TAKEN UP THE DRUMS

I THINK YOU'RE LOOKING AT THE PICTURE FROM THE RINGO STARR CONCERT, BILL

LOOK AT THAT SHACK!

YOU REALLY WONDER HOW PEOPLE CAN LIVE LIKE THAT
© 1989 Southam Syndicate

IT'S SUCH A SHAME - WHERE IS IT, CALCUTTA?

NO - NEW BRUNSWICK

"I still say we missed the last turn-off."

"They want to know if anyone ordered a pizza?"

"Our prisons are full on Pluto."

"I don't know if he enjoys it, but it makes them madder than hell."

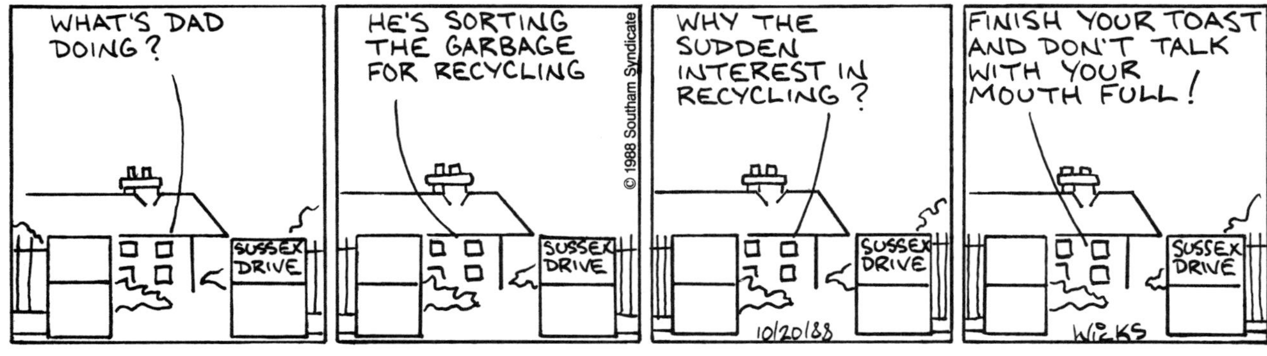

"It's your own fault. I told you not to get a fax."

"I can't remember the name but it smells like a football, and men love it."

"And don't give me any of that 'It get's lonely at the top' stuff."

© 1989 Southam Syndicate
SO, IS YOUR GOVERNMENT GOING TO DO SOMETHING ABOUT ABORTION–

–OR ARE THEY GOING TO BE THE USUAL BUNCH OF JELLYFISH PLOPPED ON THE SHORE?

WELL, SAY SOMETHING!

WICKS

ARE YOU ON A DIET AGAIN, MAVIS?

YES– I'M ON A SEA FOOD DIET

© 1989 Southam Syndicate
THAT DOESN'T SOUND TOO BAD

I'M ONLY ALLOWED TO SEE FOOD– NOT EAT IT
WICKS

IT'S NICE TO SEE MORE MONEY GOING INTO DAYCARE–

–IT'S IMPORTANT TO TAKE CARE OF ALL THE LITTLE ONES IN THIS SOCIETY–
© 1988 Southam Syndicate

–WITH THEIR SMILING LITTLE FACES AND HAPPY LITTLE LAUGHS– AND ALL THE JOY THEY BRING...

GOTCHA GRANDPA!
WICKS

"We already have a Chief Executive Officer."

FRED
© 1989 Southam Syndicate
WICKS
"Hi, honey. I'm home!"

SO WHAT DO YOU THINK OF THIS OFFICE, DAN?

WHAT CAN I SAY, GEORGE, THIS OFFICE IS PERFECT I'M GOING TO LOVE IT HERE
© 1989 Southam Syndicate

THIS IS THE OVAL OFFICE, DAN
A FEW POTTED PLANTS AND IT WILL BE ME
1/25/89

THIS IS MY OFFICE DAN!
WICKS

WE'VE GOT TO FIND OUT IF ED'S RETIRING

WHY DON'T WE JUST ASK HIM, PRIME MINISTER?
© 1989 Southam Syndicate

THAT'S NOT ETHICAL— LEAVE IT TO ME
2/17/89

MR. BROADBENT, WILL YOU BE NEEDING YOUR PARLIAMENT PARKING SPOT AFTER MARCH?
WHO IS THIS?
WICKS

"Now remember – don't go in the water, keep out of the sun, and try not to breathe too deeply."

RING!
RING!
RING!
© 1989 Southam Syndicate
WICKS
"It's for you."

I SAY PRISONERS SHOULD SERVE MORE OF THEIR SENTENCE
I WAS IN PRISON- AND I DON'T AGREE

OH REALLY, WHAT WERE YOU IN FOR ?
WELL, I WAS COOKING DINNER FOR MY STEP-FATHER-
© 1988 Southam Syndicate
-AND KNOCKED SOME RAT POISON INTO THE CASSEROLE
WICKS

HEY MALONEY! YOU GONNA COOK OR ARE YOU GONNA TALK?
BE RIGHT THERE

IN MY DAY WE NEVER HAD TO TAKE DRUGS TO RUN FASTER

WE RAN ON SHEER MUSCLE POWER
© 1989 Southam Syndicate

WE'D RACE LIKE THE WIND ACROSS THE FINISH LINE TO THE ROAR OF THE CROWD BREAKING INTO...
4/1/89

HYSTERICAL LAUGHTER
WICKS

"We can't get anything but football."

"Why do you suddenly want to be paid before you finish?"

"He's stepped out for a bit. Do you want to leave a message?"

MIDWIVES ARE ONE STEP CLOSER TO BECOMING A LEGAL PROFESSION

ISN'T THAT LOVELY-
© 1989 Southam Syndicate

-DID YOU KNOW I WAS A HOME BIRTH?
7/28/89

EVERY PROFESSION HAS ITS SUCCESSES AND FAILURES
WICKS

I HOPE OUR BOYS WILL BE SAFE IN THE GULF
© 1988 Southam Syndicate

WHAT WILL THEY DO IF IRAQ STARTS BOMBING WITH GAS?

THEY'LL PUT ON A MASK JUST LIKE THIS ONE

JUST LIKE WHICH ONE?
9/13/88
WICKS

WE'RE TAKING A SURVEY
RIGHT TO LIFE!

ARE YOU FOR OR AGAINST ABORTION?
RIGHT TO LIFE!
© 1989 Southam Syndicate

I'M GOING TO WALK TO THE END OF THE STREET...
RIGHT TO LIFE!
5/16/89

... AND WHEN I GET TO THE CORNER I'LL YELL OUT MY ANSWER-OKAY?
RIGHT TO LIFE!
WICKS

"Excuse me, Mr. Evans. Mrs. Evans is calling. You've forgotten your sandwiches."

"For the last time, Herbert, I'm reading and don't want a pillow fight."

"What does he mean, if I don't increase his allowance he'll set his turtle on me?"

I JUST LOVE IT WHEN BASEBALL SEASON ARRIVES

IT TAKES ME BACK TO MY CHILDHOOD
© 1989 Southam Syndicate

WHAT WAS IT CALLED BACK THEN GRANDPA?
4/11/89

BASEBALL!
WICKS

IT CERTAINLY WAS A ROCK AND ROLL NOSTALGIA SUMMER, EH GRANDPA

THERE WAS THE WOODSTOCK ANNIVERSARY– THE WHO TOUR, THE STONES TOUR . . .
9/18/89

AND WE CAN'T FORGET DONNY OSMOND'S COME BACK

WE CAN TRY
© 1989 Southam Syndicate
WICKS

"I'll be honest, Mr. Evans. Science doesn't want your body."

"All those who feel we should drop The Big One on Noriega, please signify by saying, 'Boom!'"

"It's Margaret Thatcher. She's threatening to replace her short-range missiles with long-range soccer fans."

"Can Ahmed come out to play?"

WE'VE GOT TO STOP WASTING TAX PAYERS' MONEY

WE'VE GOT TO PROVE TO THE PEOPLE WE CAN SPEND MONEY RESPONSIBLY AND INTELLIGENTLY—

—AND WHEN WE'VE ACCOMPLISHED THAT— WHEN WE'VE FINALLY GOT THE PUBLIC'S CONFIDENCE...
© 1988 Southam Syndicate
1/5/89

WE CAN VOTE OURSELVES A BIG FAT RAISE
YAY
WOPPEE
ALL RIGHT
WICKS

THESE POOR REFUGEES

FORCED TO LEAVE FAMILY AND LOVED ONES FOR A LIFE OF UNCERTAINTY
© 1989 Southam Syndicate

AND THOSE REFUGEE CAMPS ARE JUST AWFUL-TERRIBLE LIVING ACCOMMODATIONS, LOUSY FOOD
9/28/89

THAT REMINDS ME— WHAT'S FOR DINNER?
WICKS

SEASON'S GREETINGS

HAPPY NEW YEAR
© 1988 Southam Syndicate

YOU MIGHT TRY GETTING INTO THE SPIRIT OF THE SEASON, BILL
12/31/88

HAPPY FREE TRADE EVERYBODY!
WICKS

"It's a false alarm. Zsa Zsa Gabor is *not* on her way."

"Ho ho ho . . ."

SO WHAT DID YOU LEARN AT SCHOOL TODAY?

ALL ABOUT CRACK

MAVIS!
19/4/89

YOU'VE GOT TO BREAK THESE THINGS TO GRANDPA GENTLY
© 1989 Southam Syndicate
WICKS

EIGHT BILLION DOLLARS FOR SUBMARINES! BRIAN MUST BE CRAZY

WE NEED TO PROTECT OUR SOVEREIGNTY— SHOW THEM WHO'S BOSS
© 1988 Southam Syndicate
6/30/88

LET THEM KNOW WE'RE THE TOUGH KIDS ON THE BLOCK

FIRE WHEN READY!
WICKS

IF ATHLETES COULDN'T COMPETE IN THE TOP CLASSES WITHOUT TAKING STEROIDS—

THEN HOW DID CARL LEWIS DO IT— HE SAID HE WAS CLEAN

OH I'M SURE HE WAS—
© 1989 Southam Syndicate
3/22/89

—HE PROBABLY HAD A PAIR OF HORSE LUNGS TRANSPLANTED INTO HIS CHEST
WICKS

"He was the greatest door-to-door salesman I ever saw."

© 1988 Southam Syndicate

© 1989 Southam Syndicate

"Anybody else allergic to lions?"

©1990 Southam Syndicate
Wicks

"You can come back in, Miss Evans, I've changed my mind."

IF YOU ASK ME, IT'S JUST NOT SAFE TO FLY ANYMORE -
-IT'S POSSIBLE TO GET ON A PLANE THAT'S NOT FIT TO FLY AND YOU WOULD NEVER KNOW IT -
© 1988 Southam Syndicate
1/21/89
-I MEAN I'D LOVE TO TAKE A VACATION BUT I'M NOT PAYING FOR IT WITH MY LIFE...
OR YOUR VISA OR YOUR MASTER CARD OR THAT CASH YOU'VE GOT STUFFED IN A SOCK IN YOUR SECOND DRAWER!
Wicks

I JUST LOVE THAT OUTFIT BARBARA BUSH IS WEARING
IT DOESN'T LOOK VERY EXPENSIVE
I'M SURE IT ISN'T
YOU'D LOOK NICE IN SOMETHING LIKE THAT
© 1989 Southam Syndicate
2/24/89
AND IT WOULDN'T COST MUCH
WHY DON'T YOU GO OUT AND SPLURGE ON A DRESS
I HEAR FAKE PEARLS ARE ALL THE RAGE!
Wicks

"Hi, there!"

"The space telescope proves it. The earth is definitely twenty billion years old . . . or there abouts."

"Hey, Big Shot. It's the garage. Your car is fixed but the toy phone is a write-off."

THE LIBERAL ADVERTISING CAMPAIGN IS A DISGRACE

DEPICTING THE PRIME MINISTER AS A HUGE GUCCI SHOE KICKING AROUND THE MIDDLE CLASS IS PRETTY NERVY

11/7/88

ALL RIGHT- SO THE GUY'S GOT BIG FEET- BIG DEAL!
WICKS

DID YOU NOTICE HOW LONG IT TOOK BRIAN TO DECIDE TO CALL AN ELECTION?

© 1988 Southam Syndicate
10/22/88

NO- I DIDN'T NOTICE
WICKS

OKAY MAVIS, THAT'S IT- I'M NOT LISTENING TO ANY MORE FREE TRADE BASHING
© 1988 Southam Syndicate

ALL RIGHT, FINE
10/24/88

LET'S TALK ABOUT DAY CARE
FORGET IT

A FEW WORDS ABOUT THE ENVIRONMENT?
GIVE ME A BREAK!
WICKS

"There must be some mistake."

YOU SEEM PRETTY HAPPY TODAY, ED
ED BROAD-BENT

WHY NOT — AFTER ALL I'M THE MOST POPULAR PARTY LEADER IN THE COUNTRY
ED BROAD-BENT
© 1988 Southam Syndicate
9/7/88

WHATEVER THAT'S WORTH!
ED BROAD-BENT

THANKS A LOT LUCILLE — WHY DON'T YOU GIVE ME A PAPER CUT AND PUT LEMON JUICE ON IT WHILE YOUR AT IT
ED BROAD-BENT
WICKS

SO WHAT DO THE POLLS SAY, MILA
THE PARTY'S STILL ON TOP, BRIAN
SUSSEX DRIVE

OF COURSE THE PARTY'S STILL ON TOP! -
SUSSEX DRIVE

- WHAT DO THE POLLS SAY ABOUT ME?
SUSSEX DRIVE
10/8/88
© 1988 Southam Syndicate

OH MY — LOOK WHAT TIME IT IS — I MUST RUN, I'M HAVING MY HAIR DONE . . .
SUSSEX DRIVE
WICKS

BEN JOHNSON THIS — BEN JOHNSON THAT —

CAN'T WE TALK ABOUT SOMETHING ELSE FOR A CHANGE?
© 1988 Southam Syndicate

9/10/88

I WONDER IF WAYNE GRETZKY WILL LIKE IT IN L.A.
WICKS

"He put the gun to his head, pulled the trigger, and died laughing."

THINGS ARE GOING GREAT EH, JOHN?

HOW LONG DO YOU THINK THE SENATE CAN HOLD UP FREE TRADE?
© 1988 Southam Syndicate

AS LONG AS IT TAKES US TO WIN AN ELECTION
8/23/88

THEY COULD TIE IT UP THAT LONG?
EASILY
WICKS

HE'S GIVEN IT TO US ON A PLATE -
© 1988 Southam Syndicate

- TURNER'S REALLY DONE IT THIS TIME -
HIS ACTIONS PROVE HE'S AGAINST THE DEMOCRATIC PROCESS

EXCUSE ME PRIME MINISTER, CAN I SAY SOMETHING
8/19/88

NOT WHILE I'M SPEAKING!
WICKS

DRUGS AND GUNS - GUNS AND DRUGS -
11/2/88

WHERE'S IT ALL GOING TO END

I KNOW WHAT YOU MEAN - ORGANIZED CRIME IS RIGHT OUT OF CONTROL
© 1988 Southam Syndicate

I'M TALKING ABOUT BEN JOHNSON
WICKS

"We're about to hit land. Has everyone filled out their declaration form?"

OLD BRIAN JUST DOESN'T STOP WORKING DOES HE, MAVIS?
WHY, WHAT'S HE DONE NOW?
HE'S HOSTING A CONFERENCE ON THE CHANGING ATMOSPHERE
© 1988 Southam Syndicate
IF ANYBODY KNOWS ANYTHING ABOUT HOT AIR IT'S BRIAN
DON'T START, MAVIS!
7/27/88
WICKS

WE'VE GOT TO START RAISING SOME MONEY, JOHN

YOU'RE RIGHT, WE CAN'T JUST SIT AROUND MOANING BECAUSE WE'RE BROKE
© 1988 Southam Syndicate

OPEN UP THAT PHONE BOOK AND LET'S START BRINGING IN THE DOLLARS
7/21/88

WHERE'S MY PHONE GONE?
WICKS

WELCOME TO ALBERTA

WELCOME TO SASKATCHEWAN

WELCOME TO MANITOBA
© 1988 Southam Syndicate
7/4/88

WICKS

"Look, if we don't like it when we get there, we can always come back."

"Be back by midnight and, if anyone asks, say no to drugs."

"It's no good, Henry. You're just not fun any more."

"There must be some mistake. We ordered the salad."

"They were all out of parrots."

"You better answer his pager. It may be important."

"Pollute! Pollute! Pollute!"

"Where were you on the day the damsel was first reported in distress."

“Make like we’re atheists.”

© 1990 Southam Syndicate
Wicks
"Tell me again, Grandpa, how you and Grandma Jane swung through things called forests."

ALL I'M SAYING IS, THE GOVERNMENT WOULD RATHER PAY TO TRAIN YOU FOR A JOB THAN PAY YOU TO BE UNEMPLOYED

WHAT KIND OF JOB?
WHAT KIND OF JOB WOULD YOU LIKE?

PRIME MINISTER OF CANADA
I WAS THINKING MORE ALONG THE LINES OF SKILLED LABOUR
4/24/89

YOU CAN'T TALK ABOUT THE PRIME MINISTER OF CANADA LIKE THAT
© 1989 Southam Syndicate
Wicks

GORBACHEV SURE IS A CLASS ACT

IT MAKES ME PROUD TO HAVE A LITTLE RUSSIAN BLOOD COURSING THROUGH MY VEINS

WHEN YOU SAY A LITTLE, EXACTLY HOW MUCH WOULD THAT BE?
© 1989 Southam Syndicate
4/4/89

I COULDN'T SAY FOR SURE, COMRADE
Wicks

"You hit him up for a million bucks. I'll ask him for five bucks and he'll think he's getting a deal."

"Got this blighter out at the dump site as he was attempting to bury some disposable diapers."

"How many times must Daddy tell you – fax me first, then I'll listen."

IT'S TIME TO DO SOMETHING ABOUT THE WELFARE SYSTEM IN THIS COUNTRY

YOU CAN SAY THAT AGAIN, BILL
© 1989 Southam Syndicate

BUT THE QUESTION IS WHERE TO MAKE THE CUTS
2/14/89

WHAT DID I SAY?
WICKS

I'M STARTING TO GET PRETTY CONFUSED ABOUT ALL THESE ENVIRONMENTAL ISSUES

I MEAN, ARE WE RESPONSIBLE FOR THAT HOLE IN THE OZONE LAYER OR IS NATURE?

AND WHAT ABOUT THE PLANET, IS IT HEATING UP OR ISN'T IT?
© 1989 Southam Syndicate
3/4/89

YOU'VE CERTAINLY COME A LONG WAY FROM 'WHERE DO BABIES COME FROM?'
WICKS

DO YOU KNOW WHAT IT'S LIKE BEING OPPOSITION LEADER?
© 1988 Southam Syndicate
IT'S HELL— I THINK I'VE GOT THE TOUGHEST JOB IN THE COUNTRY
WHAT ABOUT THE JOB OF LIBERAL FUND RAISER?
9/29/88
OKAY, OKAY—SO I'VE GOT THE SECOND TOUGHEST JOB IN THE COUNTRY
WICKS

"Sure we can match you with Tom Cruise, but it's an extra fifty bucks."

"It's tragic. He was touring Europe extolling the virtues of Communism, when the iron curtain fell on him."

THERE YOU GO MAVIS, THE GOVERNMENT'S TAKING IN AT LEAST 70% OF ALL REFUGEES

WHAT HAPPENS TO THE OTHER 30%?
5/8/89
© 1989 Southam Syndicate

I GUESS THEY GO BACK TO THE COSY LITTLE PLACES THEY CAME FROM
LIKE CALCUTTA, SANTIAGO, PORT AU PRINCE...
KNOCK IT OFF MAVIS!
WICKS

THIS PHILIPPE RUSHTON GUY IS UNBELIEVABLE

LISTEN TO THIS, HE SAYS BLACKS EXERCISE LESS SEXUAL RESTRAINT THAN WHITES OR ASIANS
© 1989 Southam Syndicate

HE'S OBVIOUSLY NEVER SEEN YOU IN ACTION AFTER A CANDLE-LIGHT DINNER AND A BOTTLE OF WINE
3/3/89

THAT REMINDS ME — WE'RE ALL OUT OF CANDLES
WICKS

THEY LOVE ME... THEY LOVE ME NOT...
SUSSEX DRIVE

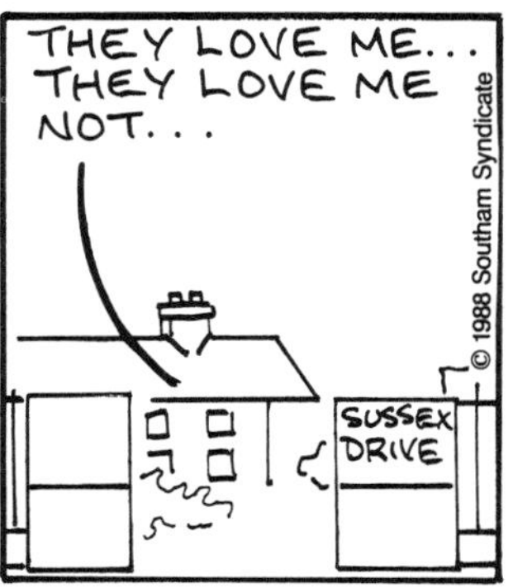
THEY LOVE ME... THEY LOVE ME NOT...
SUSSEX DRIVE
© 1988 Southam Syndicate

THEY LOVE ME...
FOR CRYING OUT LOUD, BRIAN—
SUSSEX DRIVE
8/1/88

— DON'T BOTHER BUYING ME ANY MORE FLOWERS UNTIL AFTER YOU'VE DECIDED TO CALL AN ELECTION!
SUSSEX DRIVE
WICKS

"When you said, 'Beam me up, Scotty,' you should have told him how high."

"He claims to be an endangered species. Is that right?"

"We will begin to make progress when you stop calling me 'Robin'."

© 1989 Southam Syndicate
Wicks
"Pssst! . . . Wanna buy some crack?"

YOU KNOW, BILL, THERE'S A LESSON TO BE LEARNED FROM THIS WHOLE PETE ROSE THING

WHAT'S THAT MAVIS?
WHEN YOURE IN OVER YOUR HEAD COME CLEAN
7/22/89

© 1989 Southam Syndicate

REMEMBER THAT MONEY YOU HAD HIDDEN IN A SOCK IN THE BOTTOM RIGHT DRAWER?
WICKS

AND NOW HERE IS THE PREMIER OF B.C. BILL VANDER ZALM

GOOD EVENING FRIENDS . . .
© 1988 Southam Syndicate

MY NEW CABINET MEMBERS AND I . . .
7/25/88

I WONDER WHAT TOOTHPASTE HE USES
WICKS

"Look again. Are you sure you can't find any trees?"

WE'RE GOING TO MAKE SOME CHANGES NOW THAT I'M RIDING SO HIGH IN THE POLLS
LIKE WHAT, ED?

WHEN I ENTER A CAUCUS MEETING I'D LIKE YOU TO ADDRESS ME IN THE FOLLOWING MANNER—

—GOOD MORNING, MISTER POPULAR!
10/7/88

LET'S TRY IT
GOOD MORNING MISTER POPULAR!
© 1988 Southam Syndicate

WHY DIDN'T BEN JOHNSON EVER SUSPECT HE WAS BEING INJECTED WITH STEROIDS

YOLANDA JONES FIGURED IT OUT— AND SHE'S A WOMAN

I KNOW WHAT YOU MEAN BILL—
© 1988 Southam Syndicate
1/10/88

—IF BEN JOHNSON HAD BEEN A WOMAN NONE OF THIS WOULD HAVE HAPPENED
WICKS

FRENCH THIS FRENCH THAT

QUEBEC THIS QUEBEC THAT
© 1989 Southam Syndicate

IN LIFE'S BIG PICTURE IS ANY OF IT REALLY THAT IMPORTANT?
2/7/88

WHICH CAME FIRST, THE POULET OR THE OEUF?
DON'T TRY TO CONFUSE ME, MAVIS!
WICKS

"Okay, so let's say I dig a hole for you, what's in it for me?"

WHEN YOU'RE TALKING TO YOUR FATHER DON'T BRING UP BEN JOHNSON— HE GOES APE

© 1988 Southam Syndicate
HI DAD— WHAT'S NEW

BEN JOHNSON REFUSED TO SPEAK TO REPORTERS TODAY...
10/17/88

HOLY SMOKE— LOOK AT THE TIME — I'D LOVE TO STAY AND CHAT... SEE YA!
WICKS

BILL, WHERE ARE YOU?
12/28/88

I WAS CLEANING OUT YOUR CLOSET AND FOUND THIS

GET RID OF IT — I WON'T HAVE ANY GIRLY PICTURES IN THIS HOUSE
© 1988 Southam Syndicate

I WOULD HARDLY CALL MARGARET THATCHER WALKING HER DOG A GIRLY PICTURE

I'M SO SICK OF FREE TRADE—

— AND NOW WE'RE GOING TO HAVE TO LISTEN TO A WHOLE SUMMER OF IT

PROMISE YOU WON'T MENTION FREE TRADE ALL SUMMER, BILL
6/17/88

I PROMISE
© 1988 Southam Syndicate

HERE— HAVE A NICE GLASS OF ONTARIO WINE— AND TRY AND FORGET ABOUT IT

"Dear . . . Sir . . ."

"I think you're wrong, Harold. A red-throated warbler has wings."

"No, he isn't expecting me, I just happened to be in the neighbourhood."

WESTERN FARMERS CONTINUE TO PRAY FOR RAIN TODAY –

– CATTLE ARE STARVING – CROPS ARE SCORCHED – MANY FARMERS SAY THEY ARE RUINED –

– MEANWHILE IN OTTAWA THE FORECAST IS FOR RAIN TOMORROW
© 1988 Southam Syndicate
7/15/88

JUST OUR LUCK!
WICKS

I'VE GOT A SOLUTION TO THE POLLUTION PROBLEMS IN THIS WORLD –
DUMP

– WE SHOULD BLAST OUR GARBAGE INTO OUTER SPACE

WHAT A GREAT IDEA – WE COULD START WITH THE TORIES THEN SEND THE REPUBLICANS...

I WON'T EVEN DIGNIFY THAT WITH A REBUTTAL
© 1989 Southam Syndicate
WICKS

DO YOU KNOW WHAT I THINK ABOUT EVERY TIME I LOOK UP INTO THE SKY?

NO WHAT?
THAT GAPING GREAT HOLE IN THE OZONE LAYER

THE FRUSTRATING THING IS, THERE'S NOT MUCH ONE PERSON CAN DO ABOUT IT
© 1989 Southam Syndicate
3/9/89

YOU NEVER HEARD HENNY PENNY TALKING LIKE THAT
WICKS

"Who'd ever have thought that the Sixties would turn out to be the good old days."

THEY SAY WE'RE HEADING FOR ANOTHER RECESSION, BILL

OH THAT'S JUST GREAT!
© 1988 Southam Syndicate
7/6/88

SO WHEN DID THE LAST ONE END?
WICKS

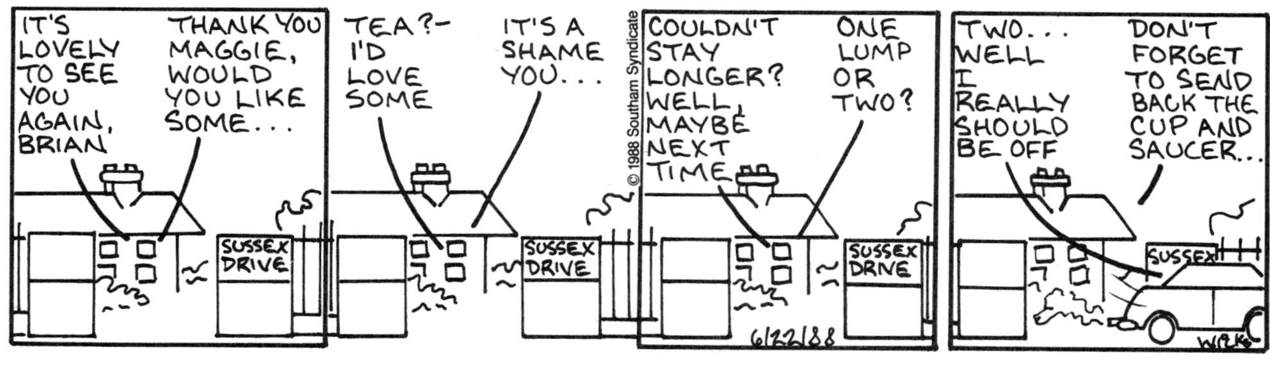
IT'S LOVELY TO SEE YOU AGAIN, BRIAN
THANK YOU MAGGIE, WOULD YOU LIKE SOME...
SUSSEX DRIVE
TEA?- I'D LOVE SOME
IT'S A SHAME YOU...
SUSSEX DRIVE
© 1988 Southam Syndicate
COULDN'T STAY LONGER? WELL, MAYBE NEXT TIME
ONE LUMP OR TWO?
SUSSEX DRIVE
6/22/88
TWO... WELL I REALLY SHOULD BE OFF
DON'T FORGET TO SEND BACK THE CUP AND SAUCER...
SUSSEX
WICKS

EXXON SHOULD BE TAKING MORE RESPONSIBILITY FOR THEIR OIL DISASTER IN ALASKA

HEY MAVIS, IT WAS AN ACCIDENT!

5/1/89
© 1989 Southam Syndicate

OH I'M SORRY BILL— IT WAS AN ACCIDENT!
VEG OIL
WICKS

"He doesn't make house calls, so stick out your tongue and say, 'Ahhh'."

"For an extra five dollars I'll turn over the ball and you can watch it snow."

"You're probably wondering why I called you together..."

"When I ask for advice, Miss Evans, I'll give it."

MR. PRESIDENT THIS IS AIR COMMAND— WE'VE PICKED UP A BLIP ON OUR RADAR—

—AND IT'S HEADING TOWARDS THE WHITE HOUSE, SIR
ALL THAT SOPHISTICATED EQUIPMENT AND YOU CAN'T TELL ME WHAT IT IS?

IT'S OKAY— IT'S A 747
GOOD YEAR
WICKS

THE POOR OLD M.P.s LOOK LIKE THEY'RE GOING TO SPEND SUMMER IN THE HOUSE

NO FLY FISHING, NO SAILING, NO CANOEING, IT'S SUCH A SHAME
© 1988 Southam Syndicate

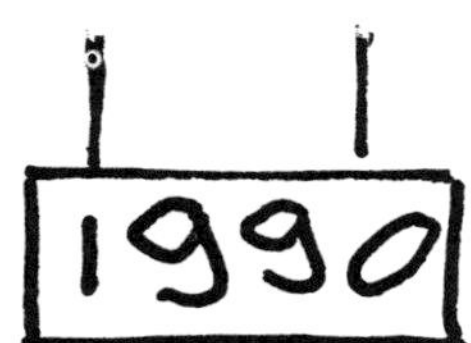

"Furthermore, it drives itself, leaving you free to use the fax and talk on the phone."

YOU DON'T NEED AN UMBRELLA, BILL –

– ENVIRONMENT CANADA SAYS IT'S GOING TO BE A BEAUTIFUL DAY
5/15/89

© 1989 Southam Syndicate

BETTER GRAB YOUR RUBBER BOOTS WHILE YOU'RE IN THERE
WICKS

QUICK MAVIS, GEORGE BUSH IS GONNA SPEAK
© 1988 Southam Syndicate

I'D JUST LIKE TO SAY THAT THIS CONVENTION HAS BEEN LIKE ONE GREAT FEAST –

– SO I GUESS THAT MAKES ME DESSERT –
HA HA HA HA
8/17/88

I HOPE THEY LIKE JELLO
KNOCK IT OFF MAVIS!
WICKS

WE WENT THROUGH THIS LAST WEEK, MAVIS

WHY DO WE HAVE TO LINE UP TO SEE SANTA AGAIN
12/15/88

© 1988 Southam Syndicate
AND WHAT WOULD YOU LIKE FOR CHRISTMAS YOUNG LADY?
WICKS

"I'm afraid I'm out at the moment, but if you'd leave your number..."

"Can I tell him what it's about."

"Try to ignore him, Sir, he's new here."

"Well, if it isn't the early bird."

THANK YOU
FOR NOT
SINGING
HOTEL
M...
WICKS

RAPES
MUM
© 1989 Southam Syndicate

"Isn't it wonderful. The Duchess of York's baby can say, 'Wa, wa'."

FOR INSTANCE-
I TOOK MY DOG
FOR A WALK TODAY
AND THIS OLD LADY
COMES UP AND HITS
ME WITH HER
NEWSPAPER

I GET
NO
RESPECT
6/20/88

DID YOU
GET MY
NEWSPAPER
WHILE YOU
WERE OUT?
© 1988 Southam Syndicate

THERE YOU
GO BILL
WICKS

NOW WE'VE
GOT NUTBARS
CHAINING
THEMSELVES
TO TREES TO
SAVE THE
FORESTS
© 1989 Southam Syndicate

YOU'VE GOT
TO SEE THESE
GUYS MAVIS...
MAVIS...
9/16/89

MAVIS?

MAVIS WHAT
DO YOU
THINK YOU'RE
DOING?
WICKS

"Okay, I promise. If we're not enjoying ourselves, we'll leave early."

"And when I ask, 'Do you smoke?', the answer had better be 'Yes'."

"When did this craving for grandmothers first manifest itself."

I'D LIKE TO GET A NEW PAIR OF SHOES FOR SPRING, BILL

HA HA
© 1989 Southam Syndicate

HA HA HA
5/20/89

BROWN WITH A NICE GOLD BUCKLE!
WICKS

I THINK THE DRUG SITUATION IS EXAGGERATED

IF IT'S SO PREVALENT WHY DON'T I EVER SEE IT?
© 1989 Southam Syndicate

WATCH IT MAN YOU'RE GOING TO STEP ON THAT CRACK!
5/4/89

AND WHAT - BREAK MY MOTHER'S BACK?
WICKS

I'M REALLY GLAD YOU DECIDED TO JOIN THE CHRISTMAS CHOIR WITH ME THIS YEAR, BILL -

- AND TO SHOW MY APPRECIATION I'VE ARRANGED A LITTLE SURPRISE FOR YOU

OKAY MR. TRAVERS, YOU'VE GOT THE SOLO THIS YEAR
12/9/88

DASHING THROUGH THE SNOW. . .
WICKS

© 1990 Southam Syndicate
WICKS
"Forget the ozone layer, what about my new dress?"

GEORGE, BRIAN HERE
BRIAN, HOW ARE YOU?

LISTEN, I'M A LITTLE CONCERNED ABOUT WHAT'S HAPPENING TO YOUR CLEAN AIR BILL

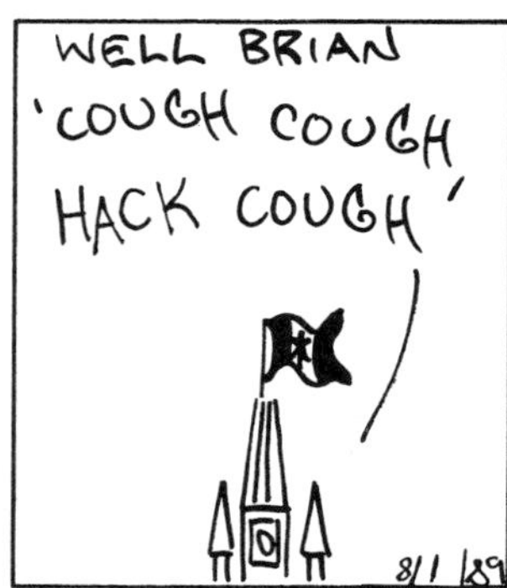
WELL BRIAN 'COUGH COUGH HACK COUGH'
8/1/89

HANG ON A SECOND LET ME CLOSE THE WINDOW AND I'LL EXPLAIN THE SITUATION
© 1989 Southam Syndicate
WICKS

WHAT ARE YOU DOING MAVIS?
WE'RE ON WATER RATIONS- NOW GIVE ME THAT HOSE!

WATER RATIONS AGAIN - HOW MUCH LONGER DO WE HAVE TO KEEP THIS UP, WHY CAN'T I JUST . . .

© 1988 Southam Syndicate
8/10/88

I'M SURE THEY WOULD HAVE WANTED ME TO WASTE THOSE FEW EXTRA DROPS

"Does he stoop and scoop?"

"I stayed single because I thought you had to wait until the right man came along."

"It's your own fault. You shouldn't have taught him to read and write."

"I can give you a Mel Gibson mouth, but you'll speak like Pee Wee Herman."

"What do you mean you have a headache?"

"Wow! You can really hear the oil."

"I've changed my mind."

"I have a funny feeling there's more here than meets the eye."

THIS NURSING CRISIS IS REALLY SCARY

IF IT WAS UP TO ME I'D GET REALLY TOUGH WITH THEM
© 1989 Southam Syndicate
3/3/89

GIVE THEM THE OLD YOU'RE GOING TO "LUMP IT AND LIKE IT" SPEECH

YOUR MOTHER ALWAYS SAID YOU SHOULD HAVE BEEN A DOCTOR
WICKS

BRIAN, YOU'VE GOT TO GET THAT MAIL OUT OF THE GARAGE, IT'S A FIRE HAZARD
SUSSEX DRIVE

COME ON MILA, YOU KNOW HOW HARD IT IS TO KEEP UP WITH FAN MAIL
© 1989 Southam Syndicate
SUSSEX DRIVE

FAN MAIL?
SUSSEX DRIVE
8/9/89

EVERY ONE OF THOSE LETTERS IS FROM SUMMERSIDE
OH, YOU NOTICED
SUSSEX DRIVE
WICKS

HOW DO YOU FEEL ABOUT THIS ABORTION ISSUE, MAVIS?

I THINK THE CHOICE SHOULD BE LEFT TO THE INDIVIDUAL–
© 1989 Southam Syndicate

–A WOMANS BODY IS STILL HER OWN, NO ONE SHOULD BE ALLOWED TO ROB HER OF THAT
8/31/89

I'M SORRY I COULDN'T HEAR YOU – COULD YOU SPEAK UP A LITTLE?
NO ABORTION
-TION
WICKS

"Next!"

THE VOTES HAVE BEEN TABULATED

THE PEOPLE HAVE DECIDED
© 1988 Southam Syndicate

THE NEXT PRESIDENT OF THE UNITED STATES IS...

VERY FUNNY, MAVIS!
WICKS

WE CAN'T GO ON DESTROYING THIS PLANET –

– OUR TIME IS RUNNING OUT –
© 1988 Southam Syndicate
1/19/89

– I HOPE THIS WILL BE THE YEAR WHEN EVERYONE HEEDS THE WARNING OF THE GREENHOUSE EFFECT

TO BE HONEST WITH YOU, MAVIS, I'M HAVING A HARD TIME EVEN THINKING ABOUT IT
WICKS

SO WHAT'S HAPPENING TO THE OLD LIBERAL LEADERSHIP RACE

HA HA HA

HA HA HA HA
8/21/89

I BELIEVE WHAT YOU'RE LOOKING FOR IS ON PAGE 3
© 1989 Southam Syndicate
WICKS

"I'm all for the country taking in more refugees, but where would we put them?"

"What the Brazilians are doing with their rain forest is disgraceful."

COME ON MAVIS — LET ME TRY AND HYPNOTIZE YOU — IT'LL BE FUN
I DON'T TRUST YOU, BILL
© 1988 Southam Syndicate

THAT REALLY HURTS, MAVIS
ALL RIGHT — GO AHEAD
9/23/88

YOUR EYELIDS ARE GETTING HEAVIER AND HEAVIER — YOU'RE GETTING SLEEPY —

— NOW REPEAT AFTER ME — I WILL VOTE FOR BRIAN MULRONEY IN THE NEXT ELECTION...
WICKS

HELLO
RON? IT'S BRIAN —

— I'VE GOT SOME AGITATORS UP HERE WHO THINK YOU'RE AFTER OUR NATURAL RESOURCES
©BWA

WHAT?
THEY THINK FREE TRADE IS YOUR WAY OF TAKING OUR FRESH WATER AND CLEAN AIR
3/24/88

WOULD WE PUMP CHEMICALS INTO YOUR LAKES AND AIR IF WE WERE GONNA USE THEM?
THANKS RON, YOU'VE PUT MY MIND AT EASE
WICKS

ISN'T THAT JUST THE ICING ON THE CAKE
WHAT NOW?

THEY'VE FOUND HIGH LEVELS OF P.C.B.'S IN INUIT MOTHERS' MILK
2/27/89

I'M SURE THE GOVERNMENT AND GROUPS LIKE GREENPEACE WILL DO ALL THEY CAN TO HELP
© 1989 Southam Syndicate

WELL, ONCE THE INUIT HEAR THAT I'M SURE IT WILL PUT THEIR MINDS AT EASE!

"I don't care what you did down there. You're not doing it up here."

"Don't look now, but the captain is reading a book about waterskiing."

"You can take my word as an industrialist, I shall do all I can to clean up the environment."

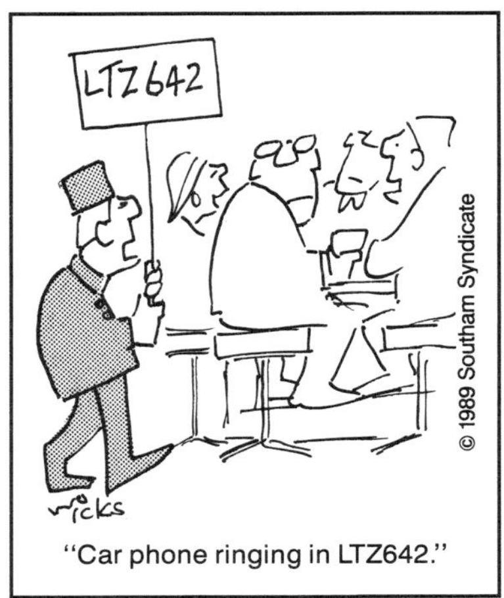

"Car phone ringing in LTZ642."

"And these use drugs, carry guns, and call themselves civilized."

AIDS EXPERTS SAY THAT HETEROSEXUALS ARE BECOMING APATHETIC ABOUT THE AIDS THREAT
© 1988 Southam Syndicate

REALLY –
6/13/88

– HAVE YOU GOT THE SPORTS SECTION THERE?
WICKS

IT SURE WOULD BE GREAT TO RIDE IN THE SPACE SHUTTLE –
2/18/89

– I'M GOING TO WRITE NASA A LETTER –

– IT'S ABOUT TIME THEY PUT A SENIOR IN SPACE

I HOPE YOU GET A BETTER RESPONSE THAN THE ONE YOU GOT FROM THE WRIGHT BROTHERS
© 1989 Southam Syndicate
WICKS

YOU REALLY WONDER WHAT THIS COUNTRY IS COMING TO
© 1989 Southam Syndicate

WHEN A BAND OF CREE INDIANS ARE FORCED TO GO TO THE UNITED NATIONS WITH HUMAN RIGHTS VIOLATIONS
3/27/89

IT REALLY IS A DISGRACE

BUT I'M SURE WE CAN FIND IT IN OUR HEARTS TO FORGIVE THEM
BIG OF YOU!
WICKS

"For heaven's sake, Mona, I said, 'Smile'."

"Sorry, no toys."

"I'm doing my bit to save the environment. I'm eating more humans."

"Frank's no fun since he got recycled."

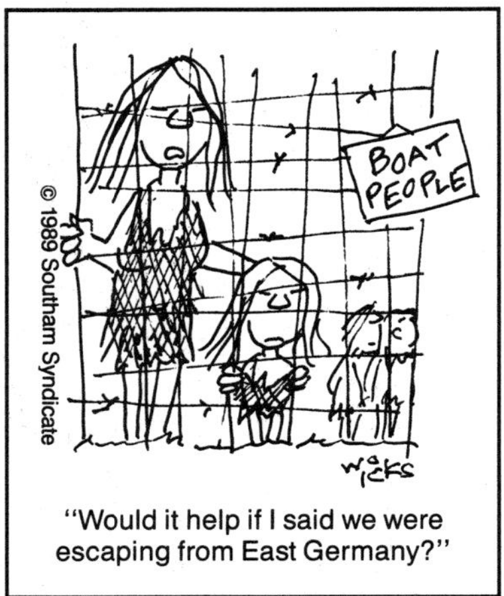

"Would it help if I said we were escaping from East Germany?"

"You've got it all wrong. I wasn't going to throw it, I was going to read it."

"The new guy, Khomeini – he's taken two Americans hostage."

"There's a wedding cake in the Bronx that needs a bride and groom."

THERE HAS BEEN ANOTHER BREAK-THROUGH IN THE TREATMENT OF AIDS

PEOPLE SHOULD JUST STOP HAVING SEX UNTIL THIS WHOLE THING CLEARS UP

YOU'RE ABSOLUTELY RIGHT, BILL
© 1988 Southam Syndicate
1/6/89

PEOPLE THAT AREN'T MARRIED AND HAVEN'T BEEN WITH A LOVING PARTNER FOR YEARS THAT IS
WICKS

I'LL NEED SOME MONEY, I'M GOING SHOPPING, BILL

THERE YOU GO
TWENTY BUCKS?

WE'VE GOT TO CUT BACK – THERE'S A RECESSION COMING – I CAN FEEL IT IN MY BONES
© 1989 Southam Syndicate
4/13/89

ARE THOSE THE SAME BONES THAT SAID WE WOULD WIN THE LOTTERY?
WICKS

SOCIETY SEEMS TO BE LESS AND LESS SENSITIVE TO THE NEEDS OF THE POOR AND DESTITUTE

HANG ON, MAVIS CAN WE CROSS THE STREET?
3/25/89

I THINK THAT RAGGEDY OLD GUY WAS GOING TO ASK FOR A HANDOUT

NOW, WHAT WERE YOU SAYING?
WICKS

"Pant and beg all you like, you're not getting the car keys. And that's final."

"I'm afraid Mr. Evans is in a meeting."

"Gorbachev has done it again. He's proposing new arms cuts with Oprah Winfrey, live from the top of Mount Everest."

"Now, that's what I call a sunset."

"Okay, okay. I get the message."

"Me? Good heavens, no! She's farther up."

"You will meet a tall, dark, handsome man who will take you for nice, long country walkies."

"All the hostages were released today, there's peace in Beirut, and Elvis has been found alive."

WHERE ARE YOU GOING MAVIS?
© 1989 Southam Syndicate

I'M GOING TO LAY A WREATH FOR THOSE CHINESE STUDENTS

HANG ON AND I'LL GET MY COAT
7/5/89

CUT OFF MY HAND AND I WILL STILL REACH FOR FREEDOM
WICKS

SOME STOCK MARKET ANALYSTS ARE PREDICTING ANOTHER DEPRESSION, BILL

THEIR IDEA OF A DEPRESSION IS HAVING ONLY ONE B.M.W. IN THE DRIVEWAY
© 1988 Southam Syndicate
11/3/88

I REMEMBER THE DAYS WHEN PEOPLE HAD TO LINE UP FOR A BOWL OF SOUP AND A PIECE OF BREAD

FOOD BANK
WICKS

YOU KNOW GRANDPA, YOUR GENERATION HAS A LOT TO ANSWER FOR –

– I MEAN LOOK AT THE STATE OF THIS PLANET –
© 1989 Southam Syndicate
6/29/89

– I DON'T KNOW HOW YOU SLEEP AT NIGHT

YOU COULD HAVE SAVED YOUR BREATH – YOUR FATHER GAVE THE SAME SPEECH 20 YEARS AGO
WICKS

"What's an abortion, Mum?"

"That's very good. Can you do any other politicians?"

"And what name does he answer to?"

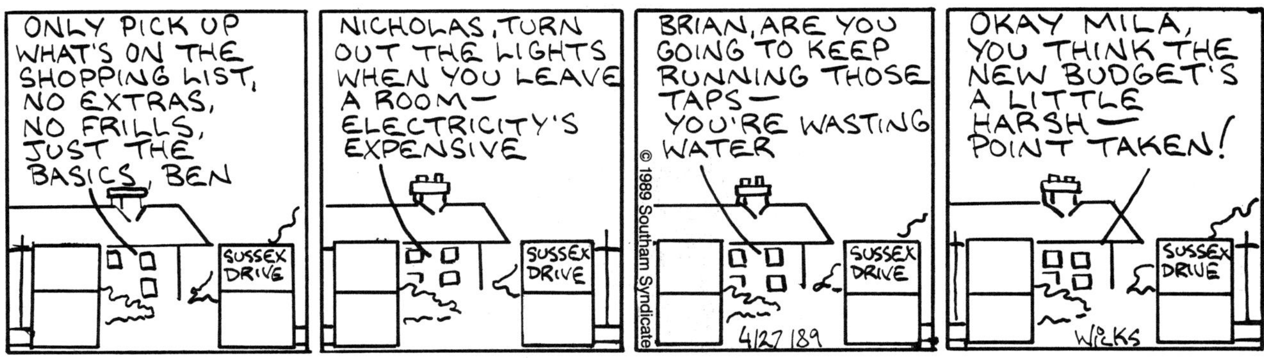
ONLY PICK UP WHAT'S ON THE SHOPPING LIST, NO EXTRAS, NO FRILLS, JUST THE BASICS, BEN
SUSSEX DRIVE
NICHOLAS, TURN OUT THE LIGHTS WHEN YOU LEAVE A ROOM— ELECTRICITY'S EXPENSIVE
SUSSEX DRIVE
BRIAN, ARE YOU GOING TO KEEP RUNNING THOSE TAPS— YOU'RE WASTING WATER
SUSSEX DRIVE
© 1989 Southam Syndicate
4/27/89
OKAY MILA, YOU THINK THE NEW BUDGET'S A LITTLE HARSH— POINT TAKEN!
SUSSEX DRIVE
WICKS

POOR OLD SALMAN RUSHDIE
© 1989 Southam Syndicate

I MEAN ALL THIS OVER A BOOK
3/7/89

IT'S CERTAINLY GIVEN US SOME INSIGHT INTO RELIGIOUS FANATICS THOUGH

LIKE WHAT?
THEY CAN'T TAKE A JOKE
WICKS

GRANDPA, DO YOU THINK SANTA REALLY HAS A NAUGHTY LIST?

I WOULDN'T WORRY ABOUT IT— IT'S PROBABLY FULL OF PEOPLE WHO VOTED LIBERAL THIS YEAR-
11/24/88

- SO THERE WON'T BE ANY ROOM FOR YOU

WHAT A RELIEF— I JUST SMACKED A HOCKEY PUCK THROUGH YOUR TELEVISION SET

"So much for recycling."

"You're lucky he's not on drugs."

"I don't get it. How does this experiment help preserve endangered species?"

" . . . and to explain the penalties for those caught smoking in the washrooms, here is our own Peggy 'The Crusher' Styles."

"You're not in the government now, Evans. When I mention a problem I don't expect to hear, 'Just throw money at it'."

"Take it from me – let him speak and by tomorrow he'll be yesterday's news."

"Aside from nine autobiographies, what else has he written."

"I'm afraid we're all out of 'Merry Christmas, creep' for ex-husbands."

"Late again. So what's his excuse this time?"

"Oh, no! Not Shirley MacLaine again."

"Did Mummy's little pet enjoy his walkies?"

VET
COOKIE
WICKS
© 1989 Southam Syndicate

WHAT ARE YOU WATCHING, BILL?
MICHAEL DUKAKIS

... OUR BID FOR THE PRESIDENCY HAS BEEN GIVEN A BIG PUSH WITH LLOYD BENTSEN AS MY RIGHT HAND MAN—

— JOHN KENNEDY AND A TEXAN BEAT THE REPUBLICANS IN 1960 — MICHAEL DUKAKIS AND A TEXAN WILL DO IT IN 1988
© 1988 Southam Syndicate
8/5/88
WICKS

ICH BIN EIN TEXAN!

WHERE ARE YOU GOING MAVIS?

OUT!
© 1988 Southam Syndicate

OUT CHRISTMAS SHOPPING AGAIN— OUT SPENDING ALL MY MONEY AGAIN!
12/17/88

NOT AT ALL— I JUST DONT WANT TO BE HERE WHEN THE GHOST OF CHRISTMAS PAST COMES TO CALL FOR YOU!
WICKS

"Stick with me, kid, and I'll get you into the Betty Ford clinic."

"I'd like something for the man who has everything but a wife."

"It's no good, you looking like that. We're not buying another bird, and that's that."

"Yesterday I had an idea whose time had come. Then I found my watch had stopped."

"Your request for a loan, to be used in a takeover bid for this bank, has been rejected."

"The village? Sure, it's just past the rain forest."

GRANDPA HAVE YOU GOT FIVE BUCKS YOU CAN LOAN ME?

© 1989 Southam Syndicate
FIVE BUCKS?
4/26/89

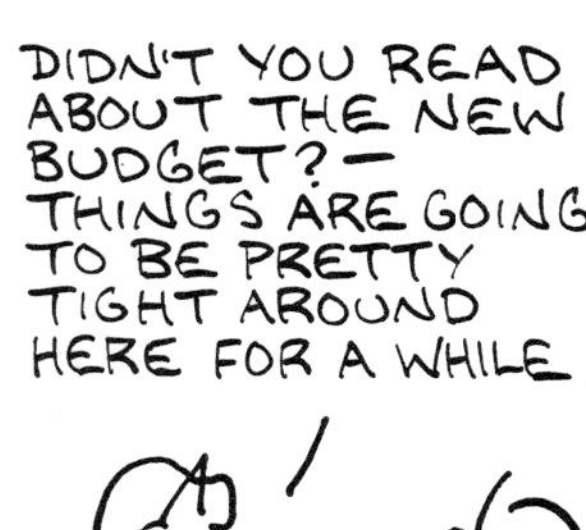
DIDN'T YOU READ ABOUT THE NEW BUDGET? — THINGS ARE GOING TO BE PRETTY TIGHT AROUND HERE FOR A WHILE

YOU WERE THE ONE WHO VOTED FOR BRIAN — LEND HIM THE FIVE BUCKS!
WICKS

WHAT'S FOR LUNCH, MILA?
SUSSEX DRIVE

I'M BUSY RIGHT NOW, BRIAN — I CAN'T WAIT UNTIL THE HOUSE IS BACK IN SESSION
SUSSEX DRIVE

© 1989 Southam Syndicate
I DON'T KNOW WHY YOU DELAYED RECALLING PARLIAMENT
SUSSEX DRIVE
3/20/89

WHICH CHANNEL IS THE YOUNG AND THE RESTLESS ON?
BRIAN, ARE YOU LISTENING TO ME!
SUSSEX DRIVE
WICKS

WHY ARE YOU WEARING YOUR WAR MEDALS GRANDPA?

IN MEMORY OF THE START OF WORLD WAR I
© 1989 Southam Syndicate

THAT WAS THE WAR WHERE THEY USED THOSE DINKY BI-PLANES WASN'T IT?
8/4/89

SO WHAT IF IT WAS?
GEEZ I'M GLAD I DIDN'T SAY ANYTHING ABOUT HORSE DRAWN CANNONS
WICKS

"You can come out now, darling. He's gone."

"Okay, okay . . . treat!"

"Now cast your minds back. The year is 1995 and you are standing in the middle of the Amazon jungle."

© 1989 Southam Syndicate
WICKS
"Did you hear the latest? Jim Bakker is selling one-week confinements in the solitary cells."

COME ON MAVIS, LET'S GET OUT AND ENJOY ALL THIS SUNSHINE WE'RE GETTING

YOU MEAN ALL THAT SUN THAT'S GOING TO DRIVE FOOD PRICES THROUGH THE CEILING
© 1988 Southam Syndicate
8/3/88

YOU MEAN ALL THAT SUN THAT'S GOING TO PUSH INFLATION UP— ALL THAT SUN THAT'S DRYING UP RIVERS AND...

WHAT'S ON T.V.?
WICKS

DID YOU SEND ME THIS LOVELY CHRISTMAS CARD, BILL?
© 1988 Southam Syndicate

UH YEAH
HOW ROMANTIC— THANKYOU

WELL YOU KNOW ME
NOW I JUST CAN'T WAIT TO SEE WHAT LITTLE GIFT WILL BE UNDER THE TREE
12/16/88

GIFT?
WICKS

"'Dear Madam' . . . No make that, 'Dear Mrs. Evans. I regret to inform you that your request for a loan . . .'. No, make it, 'Dear Mum . . .'"